OUTLANDER'S SCOTLAND

Seasons 4–6

Discover the evocative locations for a new era of romance and adventure for Claire and Jamie

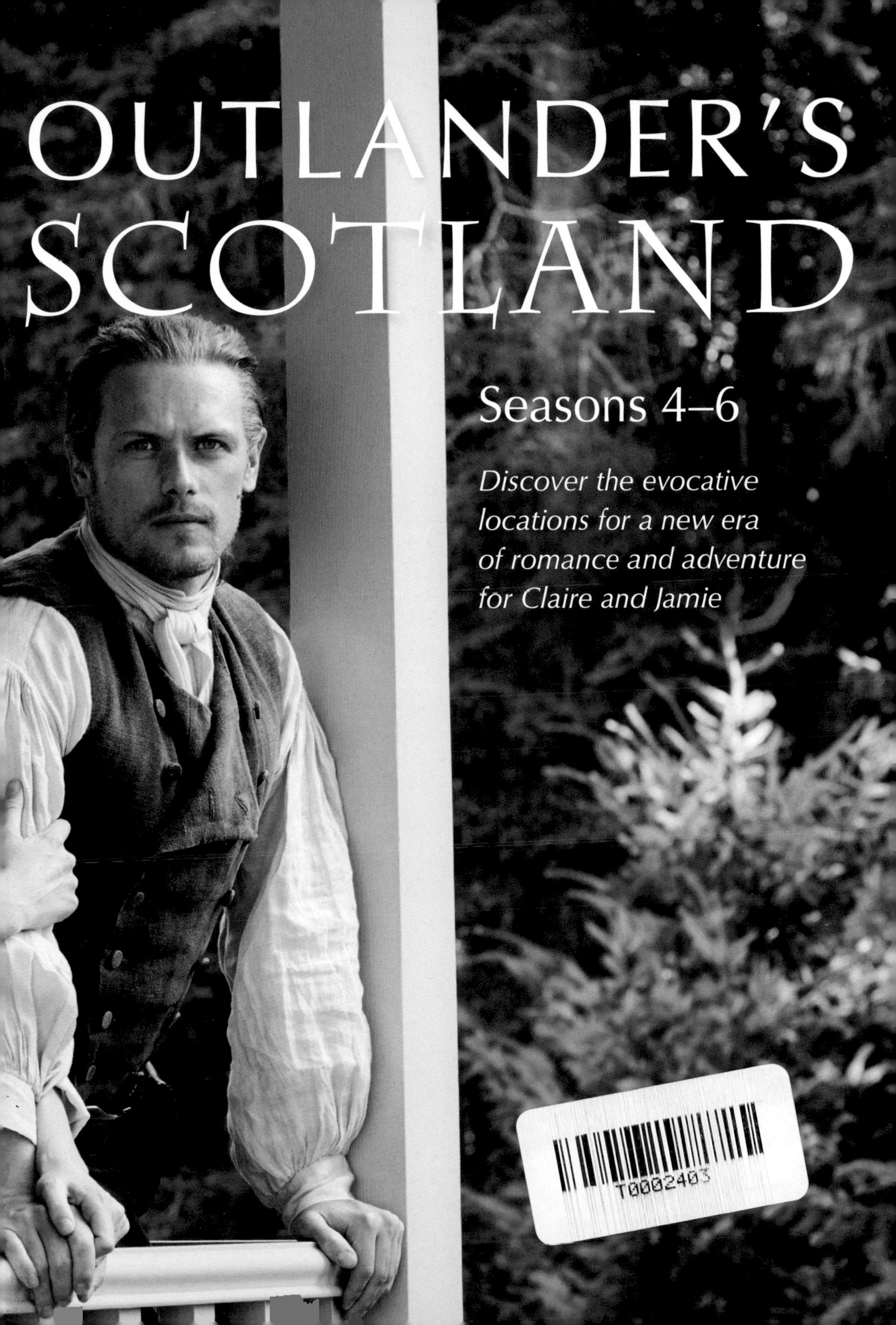

INTRODUCTION

Do you want to walk through the site of *Outlander*'s magical stone circle? Would you like to wander past the old stone walls of Lallybroch, or follow Claire and Jamie through the tangled woods? This guide will show you how. Many of the landscapes that make *Outlander* such a joy to watch are real Scottish places that visitors can enjoy.

Diana Gabaldon's genre-fusing romantic historical fantasy novels already had legions of fans before they were adapted for TV, and the shows have made the story an international phenomenon. In particular, by giving the books some locations in the physical world, the TV adaptation has created a new series of iconic places that many *Outlander* fans love to visit. The resulting boom in tourism for some previously less busy corners of Scotland has been dubbed 'the *Outlander* effect'.

Claire and Jamie first stepped off the pages, onto our screens and into our hearts in 2014. Since then, there have been seven seasons of adventures that span continents and centuries. The first three seasons of *Outlander* take place mostly in Scotland, so there are real-life castles, coastlines and cathedrals, mansions and museums that appear in the show. You can find more about exploring these in the book *Outlander*'s *Scotland*.

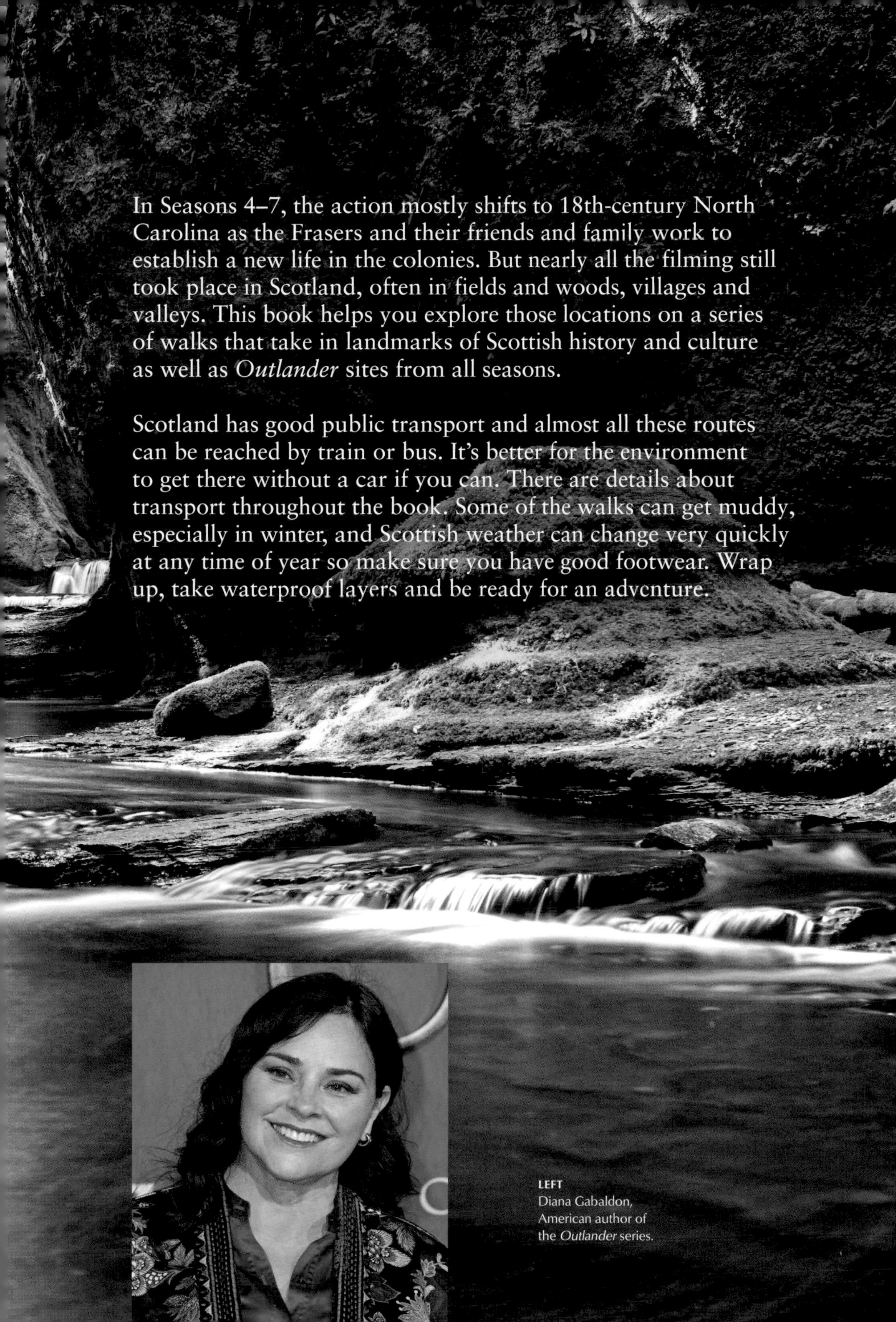

In Seasons 4–7, the action mostly shifts to 18th-century North Carolina as the Frasers and their friends and family work to establish a new life in the colonies. But nearly all the filming still took place in Scotland, often in fields and woods, villages and valleys. This book helps you explore those locations on a series of walks that take in landmarks of Scottish history and culture as well as *Outlander* sites from all seasons.

Scotland has good public transport and almost all these routes can be reached by train or bus. It's better for the environment to get there without a car if you can. There are details about transport throughout the book. Some of the walks can get muddy, especially in winter, and Scottish weather can change very quickly at any time of year so make sure you have good footwear. Wrap up, take waterproof layers and be ready for an adventure.

LEFT
Diana Gabaldon, American author of the *Outlander* series.

GLENCOE AND GLEN ETIVE

Mountains and memories

'You know my family are Highlanders. Mountains are like home to us.'

Jamie Fraser, from *America the Beautiful*

Surrounded by dramatic mountains, these two iconic valleys in the Scottish Highlands have appeared in numerous episodes of *Outlander* (and other films and TV shows too). Claire and Frank drive through Glencoe in the very first episode of Season 1. Nearby Glen Etive appears at the start of Season 6 in a flashback to Jamie's grim years in Ardsmuir Prison. The mountains in this area are the very first image in the show and the unmistakable landscapes often appear in the credits.

GLENCOE VILLAGE

This little loch-side village, at one end of the valley, has refreshments and things to see. Sam Heughan (who plays Jamie Fraser) and Graham McTavish (who plays Dougal MacKenzie) visited the little museum in Glencoe when they were filming a show based on their book *Clanlands*. The museum, in two thatched crofters' cottages, has Jacobite glass, swords and a pistol that were found on the battlefield at Culloden in 1746 and an 18th-century wedding dress.

OPPOSITE
The distinctive landscapes of Glencoe, a valley between three dramatic mountains.

LEFT
Atmospheric Glen Etive.

BELOW
Memorial to the Glencoe Massacre of 1692.

There's also a chair and some lace cuffs that belonged to Bonnie Prince Charlie. Around the corner, there's a poignant memorial of the earlier Glencoe Massacre of 1692, when members of Clan MacDonald were murdered after a Jacobite uprising.

GLENCOE VISITOR CENTRE

The National Trust for Scotland have re-created a turf-walled cottage, which faces a stunning view of the valley. It stands near the welcoming Visitor Centre with its films, exhibitions, shop and café. Walk 1, which takes you from the village to the Visitor Centre, is a simple introduction to an area that is criss-crossed with wilder hiking routes.

GLEN ETIVE

The scenes that flash back to Ardsmuir at the start of Season 6 take place in nearby Glen Etive. The prison (actually Craigmillar Castle in Edinburgh) is not really in the valley but has been transported there by the magic of CGI. The bus stop called Chairlift Road End is best for exploring this dramatic landscape. Look out for wild flowers by the path, like the white grass of Parnassus, also known as the bog star. And watch out for midges too in summer – especially if you're waiting for an evening bus!

THE WEST HIGHLAND WAY

This long-distance footpath is nearly 160km (100 miles) long and stretches from Glasgow to Fort William through some extraordinary landscapes, like the hills near Loch Katrine, not far from the spot where Brianna and Roger sit talking at the end of Season 2. You can walk a little way along this epic path from the bus stop at Glen Etive. Go past a gate with a thistle waymark and follow the track ahead for 1.6km (1 mile) to Kingshouse Hotel, where the Way Inn serves food and drink all day.

START: Hotel bus stop in Glencoe village
END: Glencoe Visitor Centre bus stop
DISTANCE: 4km (2½ miles)

WALK 1
GLENCOE

1. From Glencoe Inn, walk across car park and turn right along lane to reach museum. Continue to bridge and turn right along lane just before it to find monument.
2. Return to Glencoe Inn and walk along pavement beside A82. Path begins to wind away from main road through stands of trees and, after bridge, heads into woodland, passing ruins of Inverigan House.
3. Turn left on track signed Visitor Centre. Bus stop is on main road nearby.

HOW TO GET HERE

BY COACH: Citylink buses 913, 914, 915 and 916 from Glasgow's Buchanan Bus Station to Fort William all stop at Chairlift Road End and, further on, near Glencoe Visitor Centre, and in Glencoe village. The coach takes about 2½ hours, but it's a beautiful journey beside Loch Lomond, through glens and towering mountains.

BY TRAIN: Scotrail runs trains from Glasgow Queen Street Station to Fort William, where you could catch a local bus to Glencoe. The trains, taking nearly 4 hours, are slower than the coach, but the journey is even more breathtaking, crossing Rannoch Moor. The railway goes on from Fort William to the coast past a distinctive, curving viaduct near Glenfinnan that appeared in the *Harry Potter* films.

TOP TO BOTTOM
Glencoe Folk Museum; Path from Glencoe village; Turf-walled cottage at the Glencoe Visitor Centre.

DUNBLANE TO DOUNE

Searching for Fraser's Ridge

The gentle wooded hills of central Scotland make an ideal location for the iconic Fraser's Ridge, where Claire and Jamie live in North Carolina. The exact site for filming has been kept quiet but is known to be somewhere between the town of Dunblane and the village of Doune. A hike that links these two lovely places passes ancient carvings, an aromatic herb garden, a standing stone and the castle that was home to Clan MacKenzie in *Outlander*'s opening season.

DUNBLANE CATHEDRAL AND MUSEUM

Packed with centuries of artistry, from stone crosses to stained glass, don't miss the medieval cathedral at Dunblane. The oak pews feature carved animals and the 15th-century choir stalls are decorated with images like a bat or a thistle. A free museum in the old house over the road has all kinds of curios, from a 4,000-year-old coal necklace to the racket that local boy Andy Murray used when he won at Wimbledon in 2016. There's a little garden to the rear with displays of medicinal herbs and culinary plants, including wild strawberries, the plant that gave the Frasers their name.

ABOVE
Dunblane Cathedral is a beautiful medieval church with unusual carvings.

'Strawberries ha' always been the emblem of the clan – it's what the name meant ...'

Jamie Fraser, from *Drums of Autumn*

DUNCARRON MEDIEVAL FORT

About 16km (10 miles) south of Stirling, this reconstructed medieval fort and village of roundhouses was used for filming Season 7. It's currently only open for events, but with medieval crafts, authentic replica weapons and the battering ram from Ridley Scott's *Robin Hood*, there's plenty here if you can get in.

ABOVE
Doune Castle is set in the rolling wooded landscape where scenes around Fraser's Ridge were filmed.

BELOW LEFT & RIGHT
Doune Castle became Castle Leoch in Season 1 of *Outlander*, appearing in both the 20th- and the 18th-century scenes.

STATUES AND STONES

The filming location for Fraser's Ridge is near the striking monument to David Stirling, founder of the British Army's Special Air Service (SAS). There are three standing stones nearby, right across the field behind the statue, and one more, standing on its own at the edge of a wood near point 4 on the walk. This is the Glenhead standing stone, tall and mysterious. No one knows for sure why it's here or where it could take you.

DOUNE CASTLE

This 14-century castle with its towering gatehouse has one of Scotland's best-preserved great halls. *Outlander* fans, recognizing it as Castle Leoch, home of Colum MacKenzie and his clan, will particularly enjoy the audio guide: Sam Heughan, who plays Jamie Fraser, narrates three additional sections and talks about the process of filming *Outlander* in the castle. Look out for the marks of real-life musket balls in the old stone walls and, in summer, for swallows nesting in the ancient vaults.

WHERE TO EAT AND STAY

The Buttercup Café in Doune is one of several good places to refuel. It serves homemade food and big pots of tea. Stirling, with its castle, old town, hotels and more *Outlander* locations around the university, makes a good base for this walk. Trains from Stirling to Dunblane take less than 10 minutes.

WALK 2

DUNBLANE TO DOUNE

START: Dunblane Railway Station
END: Bank Street bus stop in Doune
DISTANCE: 10km (6¼ miles)
SHORTER VERSION: 3km (1¾ miles) signed circuit of Doune from point 5

1. Exit near Platform 1 and turn left along road. Cross river and immediately turn left down onto waterside path. Walk right up sloping path to explore cathedral and museum. Return to river and continue along it.
2. Turn left over footbridge and walk back on far side of river. Follow path up to road and turn sharp right over railway bridge, left along to Springfield Terrace. Cross near gold phone box into Old Doune Road and keep straight for 1.2km (¾ mile), continuing on tarmac path near school and over main road bridge.
3. Continue on this path for nearly 1.6km (1 mile). When sign points right to Doune, detour first into woods (straight on and soon left) to see standing stone.
4. Return to signed tarmac cycle route and continue. Cross main road and fork left along lane signed Argaty. After about 400m (440 yards), go through gate onto tarmac path for 2.4km (1½ miles). Reaching edge of town, turn left around Moray Park to church.
5. Cross Main Street into Castle Hill and follow signs second left and right to Doune Castle.
6. Follow signed riverside path beyond castle, with water on left, to loop back along wide River Teith, right up main road and right again opposite war memorial into George Street. Bus stop is left at end.

HOW TO GET HERE

Regular trains from Edinburgh, Glasgow and Dundee to Dunblane Station. Bus 59 from Stirling runs hourly (less on Sunday) to Doune, stopping at Bridge of Teith and Bank Street.

1

3

5

6

TOP TO BOTTOM
Doorway of Dunblane Cathedral; standing stone near Doune; kitchen at Doune Castle; riverside walk near Doune Castle.

QUEEN'S PARK AND POLLOK COUNTRY PARK

Time-travelling around Glasgow

Walking from the café-rich streets near Queen's Park in Glasgow to Pollok Country Park, with its hundreds of acres of Highland cows, beechwoods and rhododendrons, feels almost like going through the stones, from the modern world back to a wilder century.

QUEEN'S PARK

As the opening credits draw to a close in Season 5, Episode 5, we see glimpses of Claire (played by Caitríona Balfe) in 1960s Boston. At one point, she is sitting in a park, looks up and sees Brianna (Sophie Skelton) hurrying towards her. The camera pans out and suddenly there is Boston's Berkeley Building on the horizon. In reality, Queen's Park, where this sequence was filmed, has similarly impressive views of Glasgow. As they chat, Claire and Bree walk down a wide flight of steps bordered by lime trees. You can follow them through this leafy Glasgow park and into the streets nearby.

ABOVE
Queen's Park has impressive views of Glasgow.

LEFT
Claire and Brianna walk down this flight of steps in Queen's Park.

'And if time is anything akin to God, I suppose that memory must be the devil.'

Claire Fraser, from *A Breath of Snow and Ashes*

ABOVE
The bridge near Pollok House appears in earlier seasons of *Outlander*.

OLD VICTORIA INFIRMARY

Scenes in the hospital where Claire works as a surgeon in Boston were also filmed nearby in the former Victoria Infirmary, south-east of the park. The old infirmary had already been replaced by the new hospital opposite and it is now being redeveloped into flats. If you're still keen to see the site, detour from point 2 on the walk, left along Langside Avenue and past the monument, to look out for what's left of the old sandstone walls.

POLLOK HOUSE AND BEYOND

Various sites around this 18th-century mansion appeared in Season 2, including the bridge and garden pavilions. The wider park was also used to films rural scenes, including the grounds of Castle Leoch. If you're tired by the time you reach the park, there's a free shuttle bus from the park entrance to Pollok House. The bus also stops at the Burrell Collection, which houses all kinds of treasures from Egyptian pots to Impressionist paintings.

POLLOK COUNTRY PARK

In Season 4, a grassy area here became the site of the Scottish Festival, with its colourful tents and wicker deer that Brianna and Roger attend in North Carolina. To find the site, keep following the river (White Cart Water) beyond Pollok House to reach a large clearing in the trees. Pollok Park is also a location for scenes involving the Hunter siblings, new characters in Season 7.

BELOW
Brianna and Roger at the Scottish Festival, where outdoor scenes were filmed in Pollok Park.

START: Queen's Park Station

END: Pollokshaws West Station

DISTANCE: 6.4km (4 miles)

WALK 3

QUEEN'S PARK AND POLLOK PARK

1. Exit from Queen's Park Station onto Victoria Road and turn right. Go straight on over road into Queen's Park, up lime avenue and wide steps. Continue uphill and, just before building on left, turn right along another avenue towards flagpole. Keep flagpole and then fence on left. Walk round circular bank, heading right, to far side until distinct path leads left, down to tarmac path. Keep straight to fence and turn right onto Langside Avenue.
2. Turn left at crossroads into Kilmarnock Road. Fork right along Pollokshaws Road. Follow this road straight and then left for 1.2km (¾ mile) (or hop on bus 57/57A). Opposite Christian Street bus stop, turn right under arch into Pollok Park.
3. Follow drive ahead, forking left to stay on riverside path for 1.2km (¾ mile). With buildings ahead, turn right at sign for gardens, through yard. Turn left and wander through gardens to far end. Continue past Pollok House.
4. Turn right past café around far end of house and right again. Walk straight ahead up avenue, past barrier and bike rack. Keep straight on lane through fields of Highland cows and follow this avenue back to park entrance. Turn right on Pollokshaws Road to find station.

HOW TO GET HERE

Regular Scotrail trains run from Glasgow Central Station to Queen's Park and back from Pollokshaws West.

TOP TO BOTTOM
Bench in Queen's Park with a view; Pollock House; Pollock House garden; Highland cow in Pollock Country Park.

FROM GLASGOW TO THE AYRSHIRE COAST

Churches, cloisters, coast and wooded valleys

The city of Glasgow and its surroundings have supplied all kinds of *Outlander* locations, including the crucial Wardpark Studios.

GLASGOW UNIVERSITY AREA

The Glasgow house that acts as Claire, Frank and Brianna's home in Boston in Season 3 is on Dowanhill Street. Nearby Glasgow University stands in for Harvard. It may not look very similar to Harvard in real life, but it does have spectacular vaulted cloisters. There's more about these locations in *Outlander's Scotland*.

ST ANDREW'S IN THE SQUARE

A cultural centre in an 18th-century church became part of Wilmington Theatre in Season 4, Episode 8. The church itself has an interesting history – the Jacobite army camped here in 1745. It's not far from Glasgow's cathedral, George Square and other locations from earlier seasons of *Outlander*.

THOMAS COATS MEMORIAL CHURCH, PAISLEY

Later in Season 5, Episode 5, we see Claire in a spectacular church, fictional St Finbar's. This is actually Thomas Coats Memorial Church in Paisley, 10 minutes by train from Glasgow. She has an important conversation with the priest, and at the end of the episode, we see Claire and Brianna walking through the park again, discussing a summer trip that will change everything.

CUMBERNAULD GLEN

The Cumbernauld area, north of Glasgow, is especially important to *Outlander*. It's home to the Wardpark Studios, where many of the interior

ABOVE LEFT
St Andrew's in the Square was used as a location for Wilmington Theatre in Season 4.

ABOVE RIGHT
Thomas Coats Memorial Church in Paisley became fictional St Finbar's, where Claire has an important conversation.

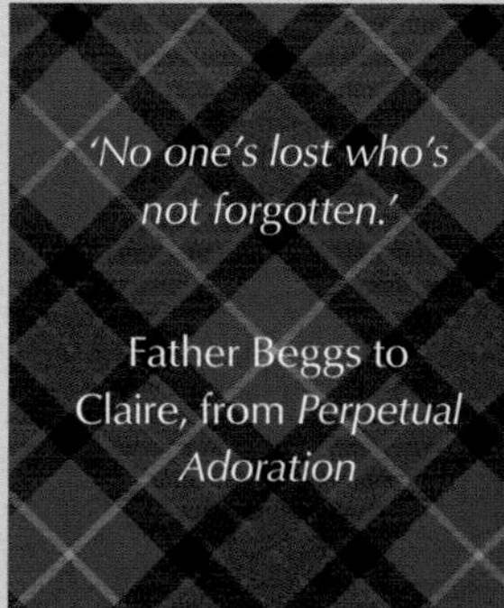
'No one's lost who's not forgotten.'

Father Beggs to Claire, from *Perpetual Adoration*

and exterior scenes are shot. Sadly, the studio doesn't (yet) do tours for the public, but you can wander freely through Cumbernauld Glen, which is not far away and was used for shooting woodland scenes, including Jamie's fight with what appears to be a bear in Season 4. The wood full of snowdrops that Brianna limps through in Season 4, Episode 7 could be somewhere here too, as the glen is known for its carpets of snowdrops.

CALDERGLEN

In Season 4, Episode 6, Jamie takes William into the woods on a hunting trip. The curving stretch of river where they go fishing, with its distinctive low cliffs and autumn trees, is Calderglen. This is a lovely, wooded valley near East Kilbride, not far from Glasgow.

DUNURE HARBOUR

An hour's train or bus journey south-west from Glasgow is the Ayrshire coast, where the poet Robert Burns grew up and where some of the show's evocative harbour scenes are filmed. The tiny village of Dunure appears in Season 4, Episode 7, as first Roger and then Brianna look for a ship from 'Ayr' harbour to America.

ABOVE
Brianna and Roger find a life together after a lot of adventure.

BELOW
Dunure was the location for several busy harbour scenes.

Jamie: This must be the most beautiful land I've ever seen.

Claire: It's hard to take your eyes off it.

From *The False Bride*

BEECRAIGS AND LINLITHGOW

Arriving in North Carolina

Walking through the tall pines and gnarled beeches of Beecraigs Country Park, it's easy to see why the *Outlander* team chose this area to represent the journey to North Carolina. It's here that Claire sees the ghost of Otter Tooth and gets lost in the forest during a storm.

BEECRAIGS COUNTRY PARK

In Season 4, Episode 3 we find Claire and Jamie setting off from River Run and heading 'west toward the mountains'. A shot of North Carolina's rolling hills, cloaked with fall colours, segues into a pinewood that is actually filmed in Scotland. Later, Claire and Jamie stop to change a horseshoe in a mossy glade with ferns. This is Beecraigs Country Park near the lovely town of Linlithgow. The park appears in the following episode too, as the woods where John Quincy Myers lives. The Visitor Centre has maps, advice and a café, where you can eat hearty Scottish breakfasts that include black pudding, haggis and potato scones.

HIGHLAND COWS AND RED DEER

In fields near the Visitor Centre, you can get close up to these iconic Scottish animals. Claire enlists the help of a herd of the shaggy-fringed cattle to help break down the door of Wentworth Prison at the end of Season 1. Red deer are also native to North Carolina; in Season 4, Episode 6, Jamie and William kill a stag together.

ABOVE
The pinewoods in Beecraigs Country Park stand in for the forests of North Carolina.

BELOW
Highland cows are among the animals you can see in the fields at Beecraigs.

MOSSY WOODS AND GRAZING MEADOWS

The most recognizable film locations, around point 4 on the walk, include the fallen tree that Claire shelters under in the storm and where she finds the skull next morning. Nearby, there's the stream where she and Jamie are reunited. The park's Highland cattle help preserve the flowery open spaces around Beecraigs by grazing them. The meadow at point 5 on the walk, just next to a magnificent beech avenue, was where the *Outlander* horses stayed during filming until they were needed.

LINLITHGOW PALACE AND MUSEUM

Some of Season 1's traumatic scenes in Wentworth Prison were filmed in storied Linlithgow Palace, birthplace of Mary, Queen of Scots. The nearby museum has musket balls that were found near the palace and relics of the area's paper-making industry. There are also original jars of the herbs and compounds once used to make medicine, like the ones in Claire's surgery. Make sure to visit both on Walk 4.

ABOVE
Spectacular Linlithgow Palace became Wentworth Prison in Season 1.

BELOW
Claire's surgery becomes an important setting in Season 5.

OPPOSITE (FROM TOP)
Path through the pine trees in Beecraigs Country Park; area of Beecraigs where the Otter Tooth scenes were filmed; views from Beecraigs; display of old medicines in Linlithgow Museum.

'I pulled open the door of the cupboard, and gazed at the neat ranks of glass bottles ...'

Claire, from *A Breath of Snow*

WALK 4

BEECRAIGS AND LINLITHGOW

START AND END: Linlithgow railway station
DISTANCE: 12.5km (7¾ miles)
SHORTER VERSION: 4.5-km (2¾-mile) circuit from Beecraigs Visitor Centre at point 3.

1. Turn left out of Linlithgow railway station, under tunnel, and follow road up to canal. Cross bridge and keep straight along Manse Road for 0.8km (½ mile). Turn right into Riccarton Drive and left, just after red letter box, at sign to Dark Entry. Turn right at end and left on path beside road for 0.8km (½ mile).
2. Follow path left away from road into Beecraigs and continue along surfaced path up through Hillhouse woods. Follow green waymarkers. Cross road and pass beacon to Visitor Centre.
3. From car park, follow orange waymarkers down lane and soon left through fields with animals. Continue along path, heading right through woods and then around loch. At far corner of loch near island, follow orange waymarkers left into trees with stream on left. Cross bridge and, later, road. Cross stream again and fork slightly right, keeping close to stream on left.
4. Reaching junction, detour right for *Outlander* location and then return and continue left over bridge. Turn immediately right (leaving waymarked trail) and follow this wooded path. Cross track and continue between fences to lane and grazing meadow.
5. Turn right beside lane. Follow orange waymarkers right and soon left on surfaced track. Keep following orange waymarkers back to Visitor Centre and then green arrows back down to road. Return along roadside path but keep straight this time into Linlithgow.
6. Cross canal and turn right beside it. Turn left at bridge and right onto Strawberry Bank. Turn left down steps under railway and right down steps into car park for museum and palace before heading right along High Street to station.

HOW TO GET HERE

Regular Scotrail trains to Linlithgow from both Glasgow and Edinburgh.

HOPETOUN

Love and loss at Lallybroch and beyond

Across different countries and centuries, all kinds of scenes have been filmed around Hopetoun House, the gardens and the wider Hopetoun Estate, which is separately owned.

HOPETOUN HOUSE

Hopetoun House is packed with *Outlander* locations from the earlier seasons. The house was built over decades in two very different styles. The older parts of the interior, full of dark panels, carved wood and tapestries, were used for French scenes involving Mary Hawkins in Season 2; while the chandelier-hung state rooms, added in 1721, became the Duke of Sandringham's house in Season 1. At the entrance to the house or the gardens, you can pick up a leaflet that shows you where various scenes were filmed.

HOPETOUN GARDENS

Different areas of the wooded garden also appeared in the first three seasons. They became cobbled alleys in Paris, grassy duelling grounds, avenues where Jamie rides with Geneva Dunsany at Helwater, and more. And, when you've finished exploring, you can eat cake in a grand converted stable block.

ABERCORN CHURCHYARD

Out on the wider Hopetoun Estate, with its grazing sheep and deer, is Abercorn Church, where Brianna visits Frank's grave in a flashback/flashforward during Season 4, Episode 7. Viewers will recognize the quiet tree-fringed churchyard, with its tall, pointed obelisks and jumble of smaller gravestones. The 1.6km (1 mile) riverside path (see walk directions) between the church

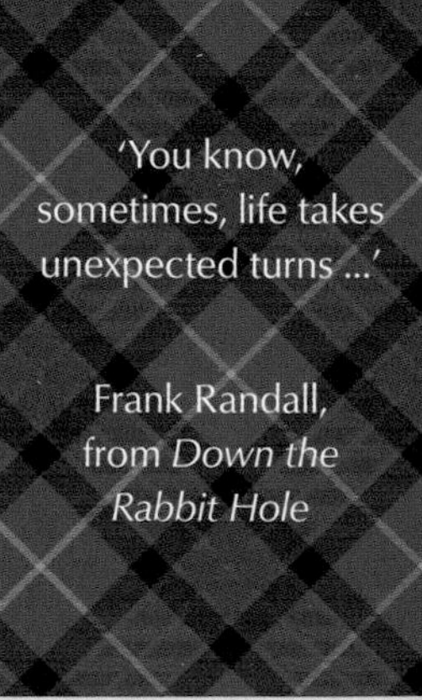

'You know, sometimes, life takes unexpected turns ...'

Frank Randall, from *Down the Rabbit Hole*

RIGHT
A view from Blackness Castle along the Firth of Forth.

FAR LEFT
Hopetoun House and grounds with a view of the Forth Bridges beyond.

LEFT
Rural Abercorn churchyard was used to film the scene where Brianna visits Frank's grave.

BELOW
Laoghaire's youngest daughter, Joan, helps Brianna get to Lallybroch.

and Midhope Castle passes the (probable) site of the cave where Jamie shelters. But take care – the path is muddy, overgrown in places and can be slippery after rain.

MIDHOPE CASTLE

Does it feel like home? Less than 1.6km (1 mile) along the lane from Abercorn is one of the most significant locations for *Outlander* fans, appearing regularly from Seasons 1–7. Midhope Castle, with its crow-stepped gables and arched courtyard entrance, is instantly recognizable as Lallybroch, Jamie's family home. Laoghaire's youngest daughter, Joan, helps Brianna get to Lallybroch in Season 4, Episode 7. Brianna also visits the site in the 20th century in Season 7. Midhope is slightly tricky to get to and needs a bit of planning. Don't expect to find the homely interiors (they were created in a studio), but you can see the distinctive 16th-century tower house from the outside when it's not being used for filming. Check the website (see www.hopetoun.co.uk/estate/outlander-at-hopetoun/) and book in advance if you want to park there. People arriving on foot can visit for free and there's the option of a lovely waterside walk nearby with bonus locations (see directions).

PARKHEAD HOUSE

If you want to stay on the Hopetoun Estate, Parkhead is a Georgian guesthouse where the garden has access straight onto Hopetoun's parkland. It is within walking distance of Midhope Castle, and owner James Gourlay leads personalized tours of local *Outlander* sites. (see www.parkhead-house.com)

BLACKNESS CASTLE

The grim, imposing walls of 15th-century Blackness Castle, towering over the Firth of Forth, are just a 3.2km (2-mile) walk along the signed John Muir Way from point 8 in the walk. Bus F49 runs from there on weekdays to Linlithgow. Blackness appeared in the early seasons as Jack Randall's fort where Jamie is flogged.

WALK 5

AROUND HOPETOUN

START AND END: Hopetoun entrance gates
DISTANCE: 9km (5½ miles)
SHORTER VERSION: 2.5km (1½ miles); follow points 1–3 using the Hopetoun House map to identify locations in their garden.

1. Walk towards front of Hopetoun and left around side of house for Ellesmere locations. Level with back of house, turn left along path. Turn right on grassy path at end and right again towards main lawn.
2. Walk diagonally left along elegant avenue of lime trees. Skirt right around pond to head back towards house past site of duel.
3. Explore cobbled alleys and courtyards.
4. For the full walk to Abercorn Church and Midhope Castle on the Hopetoun Estate, walk back to kiosk by entrance gate and turn right on tarmac drive. Follow John Muir Way arrow right again. Keep straight through gate and follow track through parkland. Keep straight again (leaving John Muir Way) through another gate.
5. Turn right on road and follow it left. At sign for Abercorn Church, turn right and follow lane to churchyard.
6. Return to road and turn right along it until sign points right to Midhope.

2

ABOVE
Hopetoun's lime-tree avenue, where Jamie sees baby William in his pram.

BELOW
Hopetoun House.

ABOVE RIGHT
Midhope Castle.

RIGHT
Beautiful waterside walk between Abercorn Church and Midhope Castle.

3

6

7

7. For a beautiful, but adventurous return route, turn left before bridge, as you leave Midhope, onto riverside path, and follow for 0.8km (½ mile). Cross wooden footbridge and keep going with water now on left. Cross next footbridge and keep going with water on right again. Follow this wooded path to track.
8. Turn right over bridge, right again, and follow winding path uphill to emerge near Abercorn Church. Retrace steps to Hopetoun gate.

HOW TO GET HERE

BY TRAIN AND TAXI: It's probably simplest to get a taxi to Hopetoun's entrance gates from Dalmeny Railway Station (book ahead with Dalmeny Cars, 0131 300 0767) and arrange for another taxi to collect you later. Dalmeny Station has quick, regular trains from Edinburgh Waverley.
BY BUS AND FOOT: If you're ready for an even longer walk, it's 3.2km (2 miles) along a quiet, mostly coastal road to Hopetoun gate from the Forth Road Bridge in Queensferry. Frequent buses to and from Edinburgh Bus Station stop near the bridge. From Edinburgh Bus Station, take bus X54, X55, X58, X59 or X61 to Slip Road bus stop, and walk towards bridge. Soon fork left downhill to find Hopetoun Road. Turn left and follow John Muir Way.

NEWHAILES

A life-changing offer

What a difference one supper can make. In Season 4's first episode, Jamie and Claire are invited to dine with Governor Tryon (played by Tim Downie), and he makes them an offer that changes their plans. Tryon's formal party was filmed at Newhailes, a Palladian mansion near Edinburgh. Book a tour to see these rooms, which are full of rococo artistry.

ABOVE
Newhailes, near Edinburgh.

RIGHT
The library fireplace, visible behind Jamie while Governor Tryon offers him land rights.

FAR RIGHT
Governor Tryon, played by Tim Downie.

OPPOSITE
Ruined shell grotto in water gardens.

THE DINING ROOM

It's night time, a string quartet plays, and we see the mansion's glowing façade. The scene cuts to the lavish dining room at Newhailes, where the guests are eating and talking. This elegant room, with its pillars and authentic shade of green, is where we see Claire wearing a simply set ruby and hoping to find a buyer

for it. Behind her, there's an ornate fireplace with a marble lion's head and sunflowers at the top, which visitors to the house will recognize. At this point, Claire and Jamie are still planning to return to Scotland.

THE LIBRARY

Governor Tryon invites Jamie to come and drink some brandy after supper. They sit in wingback armchairs on either side of another Italian marble fireplace, strikingly decorated with faces and wreaths. The same picture hangs above it in the real library at Newhailes and there's a flickering fire behind Jamie and the governor. The other rooms in the house are all worth seeing too – look out for the golden shell motifs in almost every room and baroque plasterwork decoration in the entrance hall.

WATER GARDENS

The walk from Brunstane Station passes a ruined summerhouse, cascades and grotto – all part of the 18th-century water gardens that were built here to impress the mansion's guests. And there are great views towards the sea, and further to the coast of Fife, from the Ladies' Walk, a raised bank that runs through fields on the estate.

START: Brunstane Station
END: Musselburgh
DISTANCE: 3.2km (2 miles)

WALK 6

NEWHAILES

1. Exit Brunstane Station (pronounced 'Broonstun'), cross road and follow the signs for Brunstane Burn Path to join a pleasant stream-side walkway. Follow this path for 1.6km (1 mile), switching sides near railway bridge.
2. Path runs through tree tunnel to emerge in grassy area near houses. Cross footbridge and turn right at sign for Newhailes.
3. Go through gate. Fork right on leafy path to ruined summerhouse. Follow path left along stream through woods, past little cascades and shell grotto. Follow path right to Welcome Hub and house.
4. Walk back to point 3. From here you can either return to Brunstane Station or turn right and follow tarmac path to main road and bus stop. Musselburgh, with its beach and harbour, is just a few steps further.

HOW TO GET HERE

Regular trains from Edinburgh's main Waverley Station run to Brunstane. Buses 26, 44, 113 and 124 all run back from Musselburgh to Edinburgh's Princes Street.

MORE AROUND EDINBURGH

There are other *Outlander* locations around legend-rich Edinburgh and every museum, pub, alleyway and shop has some resonance for fans of Scottish culture and history.

PRESTONFIELD

Staying at this country house hotel feels like sleeping in a set from *Outlander*; luxurious Prestonfield has dark wood panelling and antique portraits, a damask-and-brocade fantasia in a 17th-century mansion. There are huge grounds, just a cannonball's throw from Craigmillar Castle, claw-footed baths and soft four-poster beds in what feels like the deepest countryside but is just a bus ride away from Edinburgh's Old Town in the shadow of the city's craggy mountains (see www.prestonfield.com).

CRAIGMILLAR CASTLE

To the west of Newhailes, 4.8km (3 miles), the impressive walls of this huge, ruined castle became *Outlander*'s Ardsmuir Prison. Craigmillar was a medieval tower house that expanded over the centuries and, even as a ruin, is still magnificent with panoramic views of Edinburgh from the battlements. Ardsmuir reappears at the start of Season 6, magically transported to the landscape near Glencoe.

EDINBURGH'S ROYAL MILE

There are several *Outlander*-related sights and locations from earlier seasons around Edinburgh's Royal Mile. These include the outside of Jamie's print shop, where the couple are reunited in Season 3. You can read more about them in *Outlander's Scotland*.

ABOVE
Craigmillar Castle becomes Ardsmuir Prison.

BELOW
Edinburgh's Royal Mile has lots of picturesque alleyways like Bakehouse Close.

EAST LOTHIAN

Violence and villainy

The East Lothian area, with its miles of coastline, has provided some memorable *Outlander* locations, from interesting buildings in the village of East Linton to the dune-fringed beaches near Dunbar. Part of the John Muir Way, a well-waymarked, long-distance walk, runs between them and provides a rewarding hike.

JOHN MUIR COUNTRY PARK

This huge area includes saltmarsh, dotted with samphire and sea asters, and miles of smooth sandy beaches, stretching across a wide bay. Several scenes in Season 7 were filmed around here.

JOHN MUIR WAY

The country park is one of the landmarks on the long-distance John Muir Way, a 216km (134-mile) path in memory of the pioneering conservationist John Muir, born in Dunbar in 1838. Muir's birthplace in Dunbar is now a museum. He moved to America when he was 11 years old and went on to create the system that still protects Yosemite and other US National Parks.

TYNINGHAME BEACH

Towards the end of Season 5, Episode 10, Brianna is rescued from a beach with a line of sand dunes. The beach is west of Dunbar, quite a long way on foot from any bus stop or even car park. This long stretch of golden sand is often quite empty, making it handy for filming. Look out from this coast for gannets diving into the sea. A colony lives on Bass Rock, the domed island visible off the coast.

'The sea is a treacherous place where creatures prey upon one another. And the sea herself is hungry for souls.'

Stephen Bonnet, from *Mercy Shall Follow Me*

BELOW
Tyninghame Beach, where Brianna's rescue was filmed, with a distant view of Bass Rock.

'... the scent of the tidal forest, with its peculiar mix of aromatic pine and distant seaweed ...'

From
A Breath of Snow

ABOVE
Little Jemmy with his parents in a happier scene.

BELOW
The Mart in East Linton becomes Wilmington Fight Club.

OPPOSITE
Preston Mill makes a memorable appearance in Season 1.

THE MART, EAST LINTON

Outlander often contrasts moments of joy and horror. There's a classic example in Season 5, Episode 2: little Jemmy learns to walk while his fond parents watch him. The action switches immediately to a violent brawl between two women, watched – among others – by the evil Stephen Bonnet (played by Ed Speleers). Shafts of light shine through tall slatted windows into a large hall. After an act of characteristically shocking brutality, we see Bonnet leave through a wooden door. The scene is Wilmington Fight Club, filmed in the cavernous Mart in East Linton, a pretty village a few miles from the coast. In real life, the Mart has a cheerful farm shop and café in its 150-year-old building. It's the only building of its kind still standing in Scotland with hexagonal timber walls and a pointed roof.

PRESTON MILL

About 1.6km (1 mile) down the road is picturesque Preston Mill, which makes a memorable appearance in Season 1, Episode 11. This is where Jamie has to hide in the millstream from the redcoats who arrive as he is fixing the waterwheel. A room at the mill was also used for the scene when Claire and Geillis Duncan (played by Lotte Verbeek) are first accused of witchcraft.

WALK 7
EAST LINTON TO DUNBAR

START: Bridgend bus stop, East Linton
END: Dunbar High Street
DISTANCE: 12km (7½ miles)
SHORTER VERSION: Walk from Bridgend to Mart (point 1), to mill (point 2) and back to Stories Park bus stop – 2.4km (1½ miles).

1. From Bridgend bus stop, next to Linton Hotel, walk under railway bridge and along Station Road to Mart. Walk back under railway and turn left into Bridge Street. Turn right down Preston Road. Just beyond church, turn right onto footpath signed Dunbar. Turn right over footbridge and left to Preston Mill.
2. Take path diagonally across field to another footbridge. Cross it and turn left along river. Follow John Muir Way signs and waymarks for 0.8km (½ mile). Cross metal footbridge and continue with water on right for another 0.8km (½ mile). Reaching gate ahead, keep straight along track. Follow lane right over bridge. Turn left and then right to cross footbridge. Turn left onto riverside path again. At bridge, walk under main road and turn right along field edge for 400m (440 yards). Turn left on gravel track between hedges and continue for 1.6km (1 mile).
3. Reaching water, follow track and signs right and left beside wide estuary. Continue for 1.2km (¾ mile). On edge of sandy beach with row of pines ahead, cross footbridge right and keep straight.
4. When trees end, follow fence right. Turn left at sign into dunes. Follow path straight over saltmarsh and beach to footbridge (at high tide, follow John Muir Way around edge instead). Climb grassy bank and turn left with beach on left. Continue on coast path around edge of golf course and along cliffs.
5. With castle ahead, climb down steps and walk along top of Dunbar beach. Go through tunnel, down steps and follow path around beach. Climb steps to road and turn left on Bayswell Road. Beyond church, turn right into High Street. Stop for buses to East Linton is further along road.

HOW TO GET HERE

Regular trains to Dunbar from Edinburgh; bus X7 runs from Edinburgh to Dunbar through East Linton.

FALKLAND, FIFE

Back to the beginning

> 'She went to Scotland ... to visit her mother.'
>
> Brianna's flatmate, Gayle, from *Common Ground*

Roger MacKenzie (played by Richard Rankin) is teaching history at Oxford University when the devastating news that Brianna has 'gone to see her mother' sends him back to Scotland to look for her. In Season 4, Episode 5, we see his car driving into the familiar square with the caption 'Inverness 1971'. *Outlander*'s version of Inverness is filmed in the village of Falkland in Fife. We can see the fountain, the houses with their crow-stepped gables and the hill rising behind them, a scene familiar to *Outlander* fans from the opening scenes of the first season.

FALKLAND PALACE AND GARDENS

The biggest tourist attraction in Falkland is a wonderfully restored royal palace with painted ceilings,

LEFT
The Covenanter Hotel and Bruce Fountain are familiar Falkland landmarks from *Outlander*'s opening season.

ABOVE
Falkland's shops and cafés become 1970s Inverness.

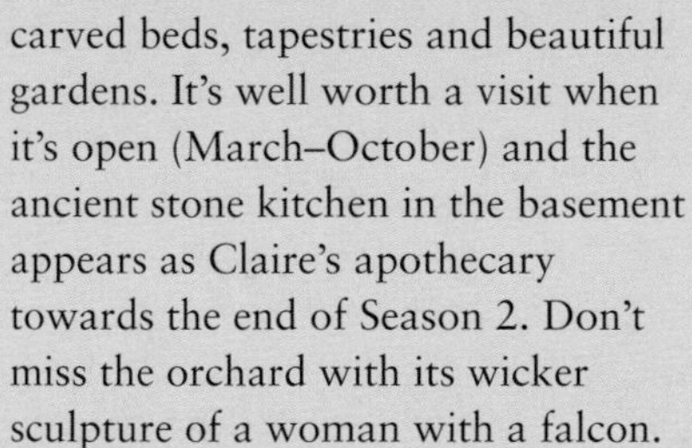

carved beds, tapestries and beautiful gardens. It's well worth a visit when it's open (March–October) and the ancient stone kitchen in the basement appears as Claire's apothecary towards the end of Season 2. Don't miss the orchard with its wicker sculpture of a woman with a falcon.

THE COVENANTER

Claire and Frank's guesthouse from Season 1, Bairds B&B, is actually The Covenanter, a hotel and coffee shop, with its elegant, pillared doorway and black-framed windows. Roger's search for Brianna in Season 4 sends him back to Bairds, where the landlady gives him a letter from Brianna.

BRUCE FOUNTAIN

In the centre of Falkland is a distinctive fountain topped with ornamental lions. This iconic location appears in the very first episode of *Outlander* when Frank, walking back to the guesthouse in the rain, sees a man standing by the fountain, staring up at the window. In Season 4, we see Brianna disappearing through the stones, intercut with shots of Roger reading the letter by the fountain with a lion's mouth spouting water behind his shoulder.

SHOPS, PUBS AND CAFÉS

Around the fountain, there are some recognizable buildings and real-life landmarks. Next to the red post box is Fayre Earth Gift Shop, which becomes Farrells and Son. This was the shop where Claire admires a blue jug in Season 1 and the real shop now sells blue-jug-themed souvenirs and notebooks with that scene on the cover. Campbells Coffee House, just across the square, also appears in *Outlander*. The Stag Inn just round the corner serves drams of Sassenach, a Scotch whisky launched by Sam Heughan.

START AND END: Palace bus stop in Falkland
DISTANCE: 1.6km (1 mile); several longer options

WALK 8
FALKLAND

1

3

5

5

1. Walk along East Port, past Falkland Palace, to Bruce Fountain and explore village landmarks.
2. From fountain, continue straight down High Street, keep right into West Port and straight to Stables café, where they have walking maps and refreshments.
3. From here, several signed paths lead all over the Falkland Estate. You can follow stream-side paths to little waterfall at Maspie Den or wander through woods to organic farm shop and café known as Pillars of Hercules.
4. Heading back towards village from Stables, turn left opposite first house on right. Go down steps and turn right over bridges onto path along far side of stream by fence.
5. Continue past playground, along Mill Wynd, and right past Stag Inn to High Street. Turn left past fountain and palace back to bus stop.

HOW TO GET HERE

Bus 36 from Bridge of Earn (see p.37) and bus 64 from Ladybank railway station both run hourly to Falkland. Bus 64 also stops at Pillars of Hercules café.

TOP TO BOTTOM
Bruce fountain and Covenanter's Hotel in Falkland; Maspie Den; wicker sculpture of a woman; Falkland Palace.

OPPOSITE: TOP LEFT
Views from Culross Palace gardens across the Firth of Forth.

TOP RIGHT
Laoghaire MacKenzie (played by Nell Hudson).

OPPOSITE RIGHT
Mercat Cross in Culross.

CULROSS

Old walls and witchcraft

Scotland's best-preserved example of a 17th-century royal burgh, Culross makes an unmissable, time-travelling trip for any visitor. Its quaint cottages and cobbled alleys, cared for by National Trust for Scotland, have been used in several seasons of *Outlander*.

CULROSS PALACE AND GARDEN

Jamie swears allegiance to Bonnie Prince Charlie in the High Hall of the palace in Season 2 and the Principal Stranger's bedroom was where Claire and Jamie stay in Season 1 when they visit the village. Culross appeared again in Season 4. The inside of the house belonging to Laoghaire MacKenzie (played by Nell Hudson) was filmed in the palace's high hall and its wonderful painted chamber. We don't actually see the painted ceiling, but the wooden walls and diamond-paned windows are initially cosy and then claustrophobic as Brianna's welcome sours. Culross Palace was built for a 17th-century merchant and is beautifully restored both inside and out. Take your time exploring every level of the terraced garden with views from the top across the Firth of Forth. Made to look as if it were right next to Castle Leoch, this became the herb garden in Season 1 where Claire walks while talking to Geillis.

'Did they send you here to laugh at me, or did you bewitch me yourself? Ye're a witch just like yer ma.'

Laoghaire to Brianna, from *Down the Rabbit Hole*

AROUND THE MERCAT CROSS

Several scenes in earlier seasons were filmed in this area. The tall white house was Geillis Duncan's house in the first season and the Withdrawing Room inside the palace became her parlour. In real life, the white house is The Study, a 17th-century merchant's house with a tower and painted ceilings. The cross itself was central to a gruesome scene involving a boy's ear and is where Geillis was sentenced for being a witch.

WEE CAUSEWAY

Just a few steps down Little Causeway from the Mercat Cross, a larger house on the left, standing back from the lane with a garden in front, was Laoghaire's home in Season 4, Episode 7. Brianna stays here for a while when she first arrives in the 18th century and helps in the garden. Laoghaire is kind and hospitable – until she finds out that Brianna's mother is Claire! The *Outlander* team have edited the view to create a more rural, Highland setting and changed the look of the doors and windows to make them more 18th-century. If you look closely, you can even see where they disguised the drainpipe with climbing plants.

WEST KIRK

High above the village, up a pretty cobbled path, the ruined West Kirk appeared in Season 1, Episode 3. The church becomes the ivy-covered Black Kirk, which villagers hold responsible for a boy's illness. 'It's so peaceful,' says Claire when she walks up there with Jamie and the site itself is just as peaceful. Claire identifies the 'wood garlic' leaves that the boy has eaten as poisonous lily of the valley.

DUNFERMLINE

Do stop off in nearby Dunfermline, if you have time after visiting Culross, to see the Romanesque pillars in Dunfermline Abbey, the resting place of medieval Scottish kings. There are some great places to eat here too, a museum, and a peacock-haunted park with a steep, wooded valley in the middle.

ABOVE LEFT
Dunfermline Abbey is not far away.

ABOVE RIGHT
Tanhouse Brae is one of many scenic streets in Culross used for filming.

BELOW
The West Kirk in Culross appears in Season 1.

WALK 9
CULROSS

START AND END: Palace bus stop, Culross
DISTANCE: 4km (2½ miles)

1. Cross road to Town House with clocktower and visit palace and garden (if open). Return to Town House and turn left up Back Causeway to Mercat Cross.
2. Turn right down Little Causeway and left along Low Causeway. Just after school, turn left up Newgate, a steep grassy path that forks right to reach Culross Abbey.
3. Follow lane left and turn left through stone gate posts of Park Lodge onto track with views across Firth of Forth. Turn right onto narrow path through wood. Exit through gate and cross lane to continue on track between walls for 0.8km (½ mile).
4. Turn right up path and follow signs to West Kirk.
5. Return to point 4 and keep straight downhill into Culross. Turn left along coast path. At pier, turn left back to palace.

HOW TO GET HERE

Hourly bus 8 from Dunfermline Bus Station stops opposite Culross Palace. Dunfermline Railway Station, a short walk from bus station, has regular trains from Edinburgh.

TOP TO BOTTOM
Room in Culross Palace used for filming; Mercat Cross, Culross; house in Culross that became Laoghaire's house in Season 4; West Kirk, Culross.

FURTHER UP THE COAST OF FIFE

'Only three large ships lay at anchor in the Firth, those of a size to brave the winds of an Atlantic crossing ...'

From *Drums of Autumn*

ABOVE LEFT
Dysart Harbour was used to film harbour scenes in earlier seasons.

ABOVE CENTRE
The tall, wooden sailing ship, *Phoenix*, was used for scenes in Season 7.

ABOVE RIGHT
Kinclaven Wood with a carpet of bluebells.

The Kingdom of Fife on Scotland's sunny east coast is always worth exploring. A railway and delightful coastal path link these *Outlander* locations along its rocky shores.

DYSART HARBOUR

This picturesque harbour became a French port in Season 2. Lots of extra scenery was added for filming, but it's a lovely place to visit. Bus 7 from Kirkaldy Railway Station stops a few minutes' walk away.

ANSTRUTHER

This colourful seaside town, with its cobbled lanes and working harbours, is home to the Scottish Fisheries Museum. The museum charts a winding voyage from eel traps and lobster creels, through sail, steam and herring markets to motors and quotas, via old boatyards and a fisherman's cottage. The museum's collection of boats includes the old wooden *Reaper* sailing boat, generally moored in the harbour outside. This was the boat that Claire, Jamie and Murtagh rowed out to at the end of Season 1 when they set sail for France (see www.scotfishmuseum.org).

BURNTISLAND

The tall, wooden sailing ship, *Phoenix*, was used for filming ship-board scenes for Season 7, while in and around the harbour at Burntisland not far from the railway station.

ABERDOUR

The medieval castle at Aberdour, right next to the railway station, was used as the monastery where Jamie recovers at the traumatic end of Season 1. It's a beautiful place and is one of the oldest stone castles in Scotland that is still standing.

KINCLAVEN BLUEBELL WOOD, PERTHSHIRE

Discover the witness trees in a beautiful wood

In Season 4, Episode 4, Claire and Jamie have just arrived at and named Fraser's Ridge. Young Ian points out two magnificent beeches growing close together. 'They're witness trees,' says Jamie. 'Governor Tryon spoke of them. They mark the furthest boundary of our land.' Jamie carves 'F.R.' onto one of the trees to show people they are entering Fraser's Ridge. These trees grow in Kinclaven Bluebell Wood, one of Scotland's largest oak woods and best places for bluebells.

This will be a sign all who pass that they're entering Fraser's Ridge.'

Jamie, from *Common Ground*

RIGHT
The witness trees in Kinclaven Wood.

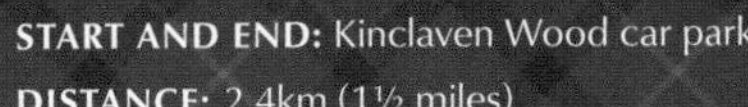

START AND END: Kinclaven Wood car park
DISTANCE: 2.4km (1½ miles)

WALK 10

KINCLAVEN BLUEBELL WOOD

1. From Kinclaven Wood car park, head past info board along path into trees ahead. Turn right on path signed Oakwood loop. Follow winding path through tall pines; witness trees on left after about 300m (330 yards).
2. Continue along main path, following arrows and signs. Continue along signed Oakwood loop on clear tracks. Eventually it will bring you back to car park.

HOW TO GET HERE

This one is tricky without a car. Bus 58 from Perth stops at Kinclaven Road End three times a day, 2.4km (1½ miles) from Kinclaven Woods, but partly along a busy road so not recommended. Probably better to drive or get a taxi from Perth.

AROUND PERTHSHIRE

This beautiful, wooded area of Scotland, on the edge of the Highlands, includes many Outlander *locations*

ABERCAIRNY ESTATES

The episodes that take place in and around Aunt Jocasta's lavish house at River Run (mostly in Season 4), were filmed on the Abercairny Estates. The grand, plantation-style house was built from scratch and enhanced with CGI and interiors filmed elsewhere. The countryside around it is real, but the estate is private so it's not easy to visit.

DRUMMOND GARDENS

Just beyond the town of Crieff are the elegantly geometric formal gardens around Drummond Castle, which stood in for Versailles in Season 3. The gardens are open until the end of October, and you can get there on hourly bus 15A from Perth. The bus stops at one end of the entrance drive: a long, fairy-tale avenue of beech trees with views over lochs and hills.

THE HERMITAGE

The woods known as The Hermitage, with pretty stone bridges and waterfalls, were used to film scenes in the last two episodes of Season 5. The woods are not far from Dunkeld and Birnam Railway Station.

ABOVE
Drummond Gardens became Versailles in Season 3.

BELOW & BELOW RIGHT
The Hermitage was used to film scenes in Season 5.

'... separated from the noise and reek of the town by several miles of tranquil tree-thick river.'

From *Drums of Autumn*

RIVER EDGE LODGES

An Outlander location you can sleep in

Roger sings a folk song at the North Carolina Scottish Festival in Season 4, episode 3. The song is known in Scotland as 'The False Bride', which gives the episode its poignant title. As Roger finishes his heart-wrenching performance, the scene cuts to an oval plaque saying 'Highlander Lodges'. The picture is of two A-frame lodges between trees. You can see these in real life at River Edge Lodges in a small town called Bridge of Earn, not far from Perth.

It's night and Roger and Brianna are walking with wooden cabins in the background. They stop outside their lodges and end up in Brianna's lodge, where Roger proposes. This is Lodge 14 at River Edge Lodges in Perthshire. Don't expect to find a stuffed stag's head on the wall, though. The *Outlander* team completely redecorated the lodges for the show. Other lodges were used for makeup, wardrobe, changing rooms and for crew accommodation.

ABOVE
River Edge Lodges were an *Outlander* location.

The Lodges' owner Mary MacKay has been an *Outlander* fan herself for years and says: 'Little did I know, when I read *Cross Stitch* all those years ago (and imagined it would translate beautifully to the screen), that we would end up being a film location.' The riverside resort, with its goats and chickens, makes a perfect base for exploring the many other locations in the area, including Falkland (see p.28) a short bus ride away (see www.riveredgelodges.com).

HOW TO GET HERE

Buses 17, 36 and 56 from Perth stop just 3 minutes away. The electric Ember bus from Edinburgh to Dundee stops down the road.

DUNKELD HOUSE HOTEL

Just across the River Tay, some filming took place in the grounds of this hotel. The estate became the woods that Jamie, Claire and Young Ian travel through on their journey to rescue Roger from the Mohawk (see www.dunkeldhousehotel.co.uk).

FASKALLY FOREST

Follow the Mohawk through the waterside pine trees

'Sometimes I smell the pines ... and I think for an instant I am in Scotland.'

Jamie Fraser, from *A Breath of Snow*

FASKALLY FOREST

Created in the 19th century as a model forest, Faskally Forest became the site of the Mohawk village in Season 4. Wigwams and other structures were created in the loch-side pine groves. There's nothing left to see now, but the forest is still worth visiting. In October it hosts a popular light show called *Enchanted Forest*.

PITLOCHRY

The walk to Faskally Forest takes you past Pitlochry's major sights. These include the Explorers' Garden, where you can find flowering glades that replicate North American landscapes. You also pass Pitlochry Dam, a hydroelectric dam built in the 1940s; the character of Rob Cameron, who appears in the seventh book, *An Echo in the Bone*, works for the Scottish Hydroelectric Board. When you've finished the walk, head to the Old Mill Inn in the heart of Pitlochry to sip locally distilled whisky by the turning waterwheel, where you can imagine that maybe Jamie is about to emerge from the millstream ... (see www.theoldmillpitlochry.co.uk).

GETTING HERE

There are regular Scotrail trains to Pitlochry from Edinburgh, Glasgow and Inverness.

ABOVE & BELOW
Faskally Forest became the site of the Mohawk village in Season 4.

OPPOSITE
View of Pitlochry Dam from the bridge; loch-side path through Faskally Forest; boathouse at Loch Dunmore; view along Loch Faskally.

WALK 11

FASKALLY FOREST

START AND END: Pitlochry Railway Station
DISTANCE: 9km (5½ miles)

1. Exit Pitlochry Railway Station from Platform 2. Before park with standing stones, turn sharp left onto path down through trees. Walk through car park, keeping hospital on right and fork right up tarmac track and right again following red and blue waymarks through woods. Cross Tummel Crescent and follow sign to theatre and dam. Cross suspension bridge and turn right on lane to theatre.
2. Continue along riverside lane to dam and follow path left of fish ladder. Climb steps, continue along wooded path over steps and bridge. Climb to tarmac path near main road and keep straight. Beyond cottages, head right into road leading downhill and follow it left under A9.
3. Fork immediately right, signed Bealach Path, over Clunie footbridge. On far side, turn left and follow loch-side path for nearly 0.8km (½ mile). Climb steps to broader track and turn left, following white-marked posts for another 0.8km (½ mile).
4. Continue to follow white-marked posts in a big circuit, past Loch Dunmore with water always on right, then up through woods and down, back towards Clunie bridge. Do not cross, but keep left under main road and through woods to café.
5. Continue beside loch with water on right and up Clunie Bridge Road. Just before joining larger Atholl Road, turn right following sign for dam. At corner, keep straight between fence and wall and follow path onto lochside again. Continue for about 0.8km (½ mile), keeping close to water and follow path to dam Visitor Centre.
6. Beyond Visitor Centre, follow signs down 100 Step Walk and along riverside path. At suspension bridge, turn left towards town. Turn right along Ferry Road and follow it under railway to Atholl Road. Turn left to Old Mill Inn. Turn left again into Station Road back to station.

1

3

4

5

KINLOCH RANNOCH

The power of Craigh na Dun

One of the most iconic images in the *Outlander* series is the crucial stone circle on its wooded outcrop in quintessentially Scottish scenery. These are the supernaturally-charged stones that cause the whole story to unfold by catapulting a series of characters, starting with Claire, back into the 18th century (or sometimes forward again to the 20th). The stones themselves are not real, but the landscape they appear in is real enough and you can visit it. If there has been filming recently, you can see – among other relics – marks on the grass where the Styrofoam boulders were standing.

CRAIGH NA DUN

The hill with the stones appears in several episodes as well as at the end of every title sequence. In Season 4, Episode 5, Brianna goes to Craigh na Dun and we see the location from new angles. With the silhouette of a stone or two and the branches of a Scots pine in the foreground, there's a view, which you can see in real life, across lochs, woods and mountains.

ABOVE
There are grand views towards Kinloch Rannoch from the film location for Craig na Dun.

ABOVE RIGHT
The stone circle itself is built there for filming.

BELOW
But the nearby Clach na Boile standing stone is real enough.

FAR RIGHT
Deer in the fields near Kinloch Rannoch.

> 'Ye know it's a queer place, all circles are. And don't be tellin' me ye went up there to admire the view.'
>
> Fiona Graham Buchan to Roger, from *Drums of Autumn*

The camera swings round to show the sun rising over the eastern hills and Brianna walking into the magical ring of trees and stones.

CLACH NA BOILE

The lane that connects the remote village of Kinloch Rannoch with the Craigh na Dun site has further beautiful views along the way. There are a few cars, but the surroundings are very quiet so you can hear them in plenty of time to step aside. After about 2.4km (1½ miles), the lane runs beside a pretty stream and crosses a bridge. After 1.6km (1 mile), it does the same again and goes on through fields of deer. In the third deer paddock on the right, look out for a standing stone. This is the mysterious Clach na Boile, which in Gaelic means 'stone of fury'.

KINLOCH RANNOCH

The Shed Gallery in the village has some lovely local landscape photographs and the Riverbank Café does great homemade food. There are riverside paths, a loch and a waterfall nearby.

START: 'Craigh na Dun' (PH16 5QF)
END: The Square, Kinloch Rannoch
DISTANCE: 6.5km (4 miles)

WALK 12

KINLOCH RANNOCH

1. Start by getting a taxi one way (best to pre-book – see below) to 'the *Outlander* site'. Most taxi drivers locally will know it. Or explain that you're heading for a track (known locally as the 'goat track') about 5.6km (3½ miles) out of Kinloch Rannoch on the road to Schiehallion towards Aberfeldy. Stop in gateway, go through pedestrian gate, and walk to little hill with pine trees.
2. Walk back to lane and turn right downhill. Keep straight for 4.8km (3 miles), over two bridges and into fields with deer. Look out for standing stone on right.
3. Keep right at fork near stone and continue into Kinloch Rannoch. Turn right over bridge and keep right past both churches to waterfall near further bridge. Return to bus stop.

HOW TO GET HERE

Bus 82 runs three times a day from Pitlochry to The Square in Kinloch Rannoch and the journey is spectacular. For a taxi from Kinloch Rannoch, try Highland Travel (see www.highland-travel.co.uk).

2

'Sing me a song of a lad that is gone,
Say, could that lad be I?
Merry of soul he sailed on a day
Over the sea to Skye.'

Robert Louis Stevenson

OVER THE SEA TO SKYE

In every season of *Outlander*, the theme song is a variation on the Skye Boat Song, a 19th-century Scottish song about how Bonnie Prince Charlie escaped after the Battle of Culloden. Robert Louis Stevenson's later lyrics, which start 'Sing me a song …' are variously adapted and arranged by Bear McCreary for each season. In the credits for Season 6, a woman sings the now-familiar lines that start 'Billow and breeze', and we see a boat sailing into a mirror-calm loch, ringed by dramatic mountains.

This is Loch Coruisk on the Isle of Skye. It finally makes an appearance in the show in Season 6, Episode 5 during a flashback that shows Prince Charles and Flora MacDonald escaping the redcoats on a rocky beach at night (possibly on the Ayrshire coast). We then hear the theme song sung in Gaelic as they row out across the darkened sea and clouds cover the moon. Daybreak shows a larger boat gliding into Loch Coruisk.

To reach this remote area in real life, you either need to take a long and challenging hike or book a scenic boat trip from the village of Elgol (see opposite). Bus 612 goes to Elgol twice a day from Kyle of Lochalsh on the mainland.

ABOVE
Loch Coruisk on a bright sunny summer afternoon on the Isle of Skye.

RIGHT
Glenfinnan Viaduct in autumn with Loch Shiel in background, Lochaber.

PUBLIC TRANSPORT

Scottish public transport is generally good. Here are some of the ways to get to, from, and around Scotland.

Caledonian Sleeper: From London Euston to Edinburgh or Glasgow and beyond overnight **www.sleeper.scot**

LNER: From London King's Cross to Edinburgh and beyond **www.lner.co.uk**

'Billow and breeze, islands and seas,
Mountains of rain and sun,
All that was good, all that was fair,
All that was me is gone.'

Lumo: From London King's Cross to Edinburgh via Newcastle. **www.lumo.co.uk**

Avanti West Coast: From London Euston to Glasgow Central **www.avantiwestcoast.co.uk**

Scotrail: Railways across Scotland – some beautiful train journeys! **www.scotrail.co.uk**

CityLink: Coaches across Scotland **www.citylink.co.uk**

FlixBus: Affordable coach travel across Europe, including Scotland **www.flixbus.co.uk**

Ember: Affordable electric bus between Edinburgh or Glasgow and Stirling **www.ember.to**

Boat trips: From Elgol to Loch Coruisk **www.bellajane.co.uk/boattrips.asp** or **mistyisleboattrips.co.uk**

PLACES TO VISIT

HISTORIC ENVIRONMENT SCOTLAND
www.historicenvironment.scot
Blackness Castle: Bus F49 from Linlithgow
+44 (0)1506 834807
Craigmillar Castle: Buses 14 or 30 from Edinburgh's North Bridge
+44 (0)131 6614445
Doune Castle: Bus 59 from Stirling
+44 (0)1786 841742
Dunblane Cathedral:
Trains from Glasgow or Edinburgh
+44 (0)1786 823388
Linlithgow Palace:
Trains from Glasgow or Edinburgh
+44 (0)1506 842896

NATIONAL TRUST SCOTLAND
www.nts.org.uk
Culross Royal Burgh: Train from Edinburgh to Dunfermline and bus 8
+44 (0)1383 880359
Falkland Palace: Train from Edinburgh to Ladybank and bus 64
+44 (0)1337 857397
Glencoe Visitor Centre:
Citylink coaches from Glasgow
+44 (0)1855 811307
Newhailes House: Bus 26 from Edinburgh or train to Brunstane and walk
+44 (0)131 6535599
Preston Mill: Bus X7 from Edinburgh
+44 (0)1620 860426

GLASGOW PARKS
www.glasgow.gov.uk
Pollok Country Park: Train from Glasgow Central Station to Pollokshaws West.
Queen's Park: Train from Glasgow Central to Queen's Park Station.

AND MORE
Beecraigs Country Park
+44 (0)1506 284516
www.westlothian.gov.uk
The Covenanter
+44 (0)1337 858282
www.covenanterfalkland.com
Drummond Castle Gardens
www.drummondcastlegardens.co.uk
Duncarron Medieval Fort
www.duncarron.com
Faskally Forest
forestryandland.gov.scot/visit/forest-parks/tay-forest-park/faskally
Glencoe Folk Museum
+44 (0)1855 811664
www.glencoemuseum.com
Hopetoun House and Midhope Castle:
www.hopetoun.co.uk
John Muir Country Park
www.visitscotland.com/info/see-do/john-muir-country-park-p252991
Kinclaven Bluebell Wood
www.woodlandtrust.org.uk/visiting-woods/woods/kinclaven-bluebell-wood